Maryland Fish Species

Game Fish & Panfish

Billy Grinslott & Kinsey Marie Books

ISBN - 9781968228644

The Mud Sunfish is a secretive, small freshwater fish known for its stocky body, large mouth, and distinctive dark stripes. It prefers to live in slow-moving, tannin-stained waters like swamps, bogs, ponds, and backwaters with soft, silty bottoms and aquatic plants. Their color ranges from olive to brownish tan. They are usually small, rarely exceeding 6 to 8 inches in length.

The Blue spotted sunfish is a small freshwater fish known for its vibrant blue spots and tolerance for acidic low oxygen waters. They are native to the southeastern and eastern United States, inhabiting ponds, rivers, and backwaters with dense vegetation. They are one of the smallest fish in their family, typically reaching a maximum length of about 3.7 inches. Both males and females have light blue or white spots, but males tend to have more intense and vibrant spotting. They have a relatively short lifespan, typically living around 5 years.

Longear sunfish are small, thin-bodied fish with a unique long ear flap on their gill cover, that how they got their name long ear. They are often mistaken for a pumpkinseed. They have an olive to rusty-brown back, a bright orange belly. They typically reach a length of 4.5 inches. They are mostly active during the day and inactive at night.

The Blue spotted sunfish is a small freshwater fish known for its vibrant blue spots and tolerance for acidic low oxygen waters. They are native to the southeastern and eastern United States, inhabiting ponds, rivers, and backwaters with dense vegetation. They are one of the smallest fish in their family, typically reaching a maximum length of about 3.7 inches. Both males and females have light blue or white spots, but males tend to have more intense and vibrant spotting. They have a relatively short lifespan, typically living around 5 years.

Longear sunfish are small, thin-bodied fish with a unique long ear flap on their gill cover, that how they got their name long ear. They are often mistaken for a pumpkinseed. They have an olive to rusty-brown back, a bright orange belly. They typically reach a length of 4.5 inches. They are mostly active during the day and inactive at night.

The Flier is a small, sunfish known for its olive-green color, rows of dark spots, and a dark teardrop or streak below its eye, with large dorsal and anal fins. It inhabits slow-moving, clear waters in the Southern U.S. coastal plains and Mississippi river basin. They feed on insects, snails, worms, leeches, crustaceans, and small fish, also some phytoplankton.

Redear sunfish are known for their red or orange-edged gill flaps. They are a type of sunfish that thrive in warm, quiet waters, feeding primarily on mollusks and snails, and can grow up to 12 inches and weigh as much as 2 pounds. They are also known as shellcracker, due to their diet and the way they crush shells. The redear sunfish will thrive in most warm-water lakes and streams.

The Warmouth is a member of the Rock Bass, Green Sunfish and Bluegill family. They can survive in low oxygen environments while other fish cannot. Warmouth can thrive in muddy water, when other fish can't. Warmouth are often confused with rock bass. The difference between the two is in the anal fin: warmouth have three spines on the anal fin ray and rock bass have six spines.

Banded Sunfish got their name because they have darker lines that run vertically on their sides. They also have a rounded tail with spots on their body, tail and fins. Banded sunfish are typically only about 2 inches long, making them one of the smallest sunfish. Their small size makes them vulnerable to larger fish, so they thrive in protected areas. Banded sunfish prefer slow-moving, vegetated waters like swamps, ponds, and backwaters of creeks.

The Green Sunfish is blue green in color. It has yellow flecks on both its scales and some parts of its sides. The Green Sunfish also has broken blue stripes which is why some people confuse it with the Bluegill. Green Sunfish are very adaptable. They can live in any body of water that has vegetation or weeds. Green sunfish are opportunistic feeders, consuming insects, small fish, and other invertebrates.

The bluegill also considered a sunfish is the most popular fish to fish for. They are called pan fish because they are about the size of a frying pan. Bluegills love to eat insects and bugs. They have good vision and rely on their keen eyesight to feed. Three types in this group are the Bluegill, Sunfish, and Pumpkinseed.

The Redbreast sunfish has a red-yellow chest and belly with rusty brown spots on their body. The species is known for its distinctive grunting vocalizations, which are produced by grinding their teeth together. Redbreast sunfish can survive in oxygen-poor environments by using their gills to extract oxygen from air bubbles trapped in aquatic vegetation.

Hybrid sunfish are fast-growing crosses between two different sunfish species. Often found in lakes and ponds where both species coexist, these hybrids are known for being aggressive fighters and often grow larger than their parent species. Some of the hybrids are Pumpkingill, (pumpkinseed and a bluegill), Greengill, (bluegill and green sunfish)

The Pumpkinseed is also known as pond perch, sun perch, and punky's sunfish. It can be found in numerous lakes, ponds, and rivers. It is their body shape resembling the seed of a pumpkin, that inspired their name. Pumpkinseed sunfish have speckles on their orangish colored sides and back, with a yellow to orange belly and chest. They are active during the day and rest at night near the bottom or in shelter areas.

White perch grow seven to ten inches in length and rarely weigh more than one pound. They have a silvery body with faint lines on the sides. The white perch is an opportunistic feeder. Young feed primarily on zooplankton and adults feed on aquatic insect larvae, minnows and fish eggs. White Perch is a euryhaline species, inhabiting fresh, brackish and coastal waters. The largest White perch caught in Maryland, is a 1.9-pound fish.

The two most famous perches are the common perch and the yellow perch. The yellow perch has a brilliant greenish yellow color with orange fins. The yellow perch is the biggest one and can grow to a size of 18 inches. It's also known as the jumbo perch. The other type of perch is the white perch. The largest yellow perch caught in Maryland is a 2.3-pound, 16-inch fish.

Alewives are anadromous fish that migrate from the ocean to freshwater rivers and streams to spawn. They are small, silvery herring-like fish with a saw-edged belly and a forked tail. Alewives have a distinctive saw-edge on their belly, formed by modified scales called scutes. This feature is used for protection and is also what gives them the nickname saw bellies. While most alewives are anadromous, there are also populations that have become landlocked.

Fallfish are the largest native minnow species in eastern North America, often reaching 15-18 inches in length and weighing over 2 pounds, inhabiting clear, rocky streams. They are known for building massive, pyramid-shaped nests from rocks, with males creating structures that can reach 6 feet in diameter and weigh up to 2 tons. They are silvery with dark-edged scales, a dark stripe along the back, and a large, blunt snout. The largest Fallfish caught in Maryland is a 3.2-pound fish.

Rock bass are common, aggressive, red-eyed panfish often mistaken for young smallmouth bass The Rock Bass is not actually a bass but a member of the sunfish family. The biggest Rock Bass ever caught on record weighs about three pounds and was a little over one foot long. Rock bass, like waters with rocky vegetated areas, that's how they got their name.

There are two main types of crappies. The white crappie and the black crappie. They are also members of the sunfish family. The difference between the white and black crappie is one has dark spots and the other has dark lines and is lighter in color. The white crappie has six dorsal fin spines, whereas the black crappie has eight dorsal fin spines. The white crappie can grow bigger and more of the bigger white crappie are caught in North America. The biggest crappie caught in Maryland was 17 inches long.

The white sucker fish has the same mouth as a carp. They got their name because their mouth is like a suction cup. They normally are bottom feeders and suck their food from the bottom of the lake. Many people use sucker fish to fish for northern pike and other big game fish. A notable large white sucker caught in Maryland was a 21-inch, 3.45-lb fish.

The Longnose Sucker is recognized by its long snout, cylindrical body, and thick, papillose lips. They have a dusky gray green to brown back with a white, underside, and a distinctive long snout that overhangs the mouth. Typically, they grow 12 to 18 inches long and live 8 to 20 years. Longnose suckers are bottom feeders that use their fleshy lips to vacuum up algae, midge larvae, small mollusks, and various aquatic invertebrates.

The shorthead redhorse is a sucker fish, recognized by its olive-green back, golden sides, and distinctive red tail. Thriving in swift, clear-to-cloudy rivers and lakes with gravel/sand bottoms, they feed on insects and mollusks. They are primarily bottom feeders. They are often found in groups, feeding in fast-moving water known as riffles. Generally, they are 9-18 inches in length, weighing 1-3 pounds. But they can grow up to 2 feet long and reach up to 5 pounds.

The golden redhorse is a freshwater fish in the sucker family, commonly identified by its bronze-gold sides, white belly, and slate-gray tail. Averaging 12–18 inches and 1–2 pounds, they inhabit clear to moderately turbid rivers and streams with gravel bottoms. They are known to form schools and are generally more tolerant of poor environmental conditions than other redhorse species. As bottom-feeders, they consume larval midges, mayflies, caddisflies, other invertebrates, and algae.

The creek chubsucker is a small (4–14 inches), slender, freshwater fish. They are olive-brown on top with a golden-yellow belly, often featuring dark, cross-hatched scales and a dark lateral band. Unlike other suckers, they have a V-shaped lower lip. They prefer clear, slow-moving streams with sand-gravel-mud bottoms. As bottom-feeders, they consume small aquatic insects, and algae.

Mottled sculpins are small, bottom-dwelling fish with a flattened body shape, large pectoral fins, and a unique camouflage pattern, often found in clear, fast-flowing waters with rocky substrates, and they are known for their ambush hunting tactics. Sculpins have very large mouths and can swallow items nearly as large as themselves. Many sculpins have venomous spines along their fins, with particularly dangerous spines on their gill covers, used for defense.

The black, brown and yellow bullhead are part of the catfish family. They usually only grow to about 10 inches long. They use their whiskers to help find food. The bullhead is the most common member of the catfish family. Bullheads live in the water containing low oxygen levels. They can survive on low oxygen areas, where other fish can't. The largest bullhead catfish caught in Maryland is a 4.94-pound fish.

The stonecat is a slender, freshwater catfish known for its preference for living in fast moving streams and rivers. They are often found under rocks and boulders in riffles. Stonecats have a long, thin body with a rounded or slightly forked tail. Their color varies, typically ranging from tan to gray on the back and sides, with a lighter belly. Stonecats are primarily active at night, feeding on insects, fish eggs, and small fish.

The Channel Catfish are the most fished catfish species with around 8 million anglers fishing for them per year. Channel catfish have taste buds all over their body, making them highly sensitive to the taste and smell of food. They also have barbels (whiskers) around their mouths, which are used for sensing and tasting food. They use sound waves to communicate with each other. They can also produce alarm substances to warn other catfish of danger. The largest channel catfish caught in Maryland was a 29-pound, 10-ounce fish.

The madtom is a small catfish that is native to the eastern United States. Madtoms are scaleless fishes with eight whisker-like barbels around their mouths used as sensors. The madtom feeds on the bottom at night, using its sensitive barbels, whiskers to touch and taste for food. Its diet consists mostly of aquatic insects.

White catfish are interesting because they are smaller than other common catfish species like channel catfish, they have a wider head and lack the black spots of channel catfish. White catfish are the smallest of the large North American catfish species. The White catfish has white chin barbells, which distinguish it from other species. There are four pairs of barbels, whiskers around the mouth, two on the chin, one at the angle of the mouth, and one behind the nostril. The largest White Catfish caught in Maryland was a 9.61-pound fish.

Flathead Catfish, their body is wide but flattened and very low in height. Both eyes are on the top of the flattened head, giving them excellent vision to see upward. Flathead catfish prefer deep, slow-moving rivers, lakes, and reservoirs, often hiding under banks, log jams, and in brush piles. Mostly solitary and nocturnal, they move from deep water to shallower areas at night. The largest flathead catfish caught in Maryland is a 57-pound, 50-inch-long fish.

Blue catfish are North America's largest catfish, often exceeding 100 pounds and 5 feet in length. They prefer large, deep, fast-flowing rivers with sandy bottoms. Blue catfish, like other catfish, lack scales and have smooth skin. They have barbels (whiskers) around their mouths, which are used for sensing and tasting food. They are generally slate blue on the back and silvery/white on the underside. The largest blue catfish ever caught in Maryland is an 84-pound fish.

Bowfins can breathe both air and water, putting them at an advantage in low-oxygen waters. Bowfins are often described as prehistoric relics. This is because species can be traced to fossils from the Cretaceous, Eocene and Jurassic period. Bowfin typically reach 20–28 inches in length and weigh 4–10 pounds, though they can grow up to 43 inches and over 20 pounds.

The American shad is the largest species in the herring family. They are known for a delicate, rich flavor, often described as oily or like sardines. They can grow up to 30 inches and weigh up to 12 pounds. They have a metallic blue/green back, silver sides, a deeply forked tail, and a row of dark spots behind the gill flap. They prefer freshwater rivers for spawning and the Atlantic Ocean for feeding, often traveling hundreds of miles upstream. The largest American shad on record in Maryland weighed 8.1 pounds.

Striped bass are often called Stripers. Striped bass live in both salt and fresh water. Striped bass have very sensitive eyes and will seek deep water when the sun is out. Striped bass have a preferred water temperature range of from 55° F to 68° F, and swim to find water of these temperatures. White Bass are related to Striped Bass and have lighter stripes on their sides. The largest striped bass (rockfish) ever caught in Maryland is a 67-pound, 8-ounce fish.

Sturgeons have sharp spines on their back, so be careful when handling them. Instead of scales, sturgeon skin is covered in bony plates called scutes, which can be very sharp on young sturgeon. Sturgeons have been around since the dinosaur days. Sturgeons mostly live in large, freshwater lakes and rivers. Their average lifespan is 50 to 60 years. The largest Atlantic sturgeon recorded in a Maryland measured just under 7 feet 10 inches long and weighed over 200 pounds.

There are few different species of Gar, the Longnose gar, Short nose and Alligator gar. The Long Nose Gar got its name because of its long mouth that looks like an alligator's mouth. The alligator gar is one of the biggest freshwater fish growing up to 10 feet long. The world record for a catch was set at 327 pounds. The largest Longnose Gar ever caught in Maryland is a 20.5-pound fish (49.5 inches long).

The American eel is North America's only freshwater eel, known for its snake-like body, and ability to live in freshwater. They have a Snake-like body, dark on top (green/brown) with yellowish sides and a pale belly. They have a continuous fin that runs along the length of their whole back. They use their whole body to swim and can slither like a snake over the ground and obstacles. They are most active at night and hide during the day, under rocks or burying themselves into the sediment at the bottom. The largest American eel recorded in Maryland weighed 3 pounds 11.68 ounces and measured 36 inches in length.

Snakehead fish are known as walking fish, because they can move on
land for days by wiggling with their fins and body. They can breathe air
with lung-like organs, allowing them to survive out of water for days
and even crawl to new water bodies using their fins. They can also
burrow into the mud and hibernate during cold weather or dry spells.
They thrive in various slow-moving, shallow, vegetated waters, like
ponds, swamps, and streams, and can survive in low oxygen levels. The
largest Northern snakehead fish ever caught in Maryland weighed 21.8
pounds.

Male freshwater drum also known as sheepshead make a rumbling or grunting sound by contracting muscles along their air bladder walls. They have large, ivory-like ear bones that can be up to an inch in diameter, which Native Americans used as necklaces or bracelets and sometimes referred to as the lucky stones. Freshwater drum are primarily bottom feeders, spending much of their time near the bottom of lakes and rivers in search of food. The largest freshwater drum documented in the Maryland weighed 17 pounds 10 ounces.

Carp have bronze-gold scales, a long dorsal fin, and two pairs of distinctive barbels (whiskers) near their mouth. Carp have long been an important food fish to humans. Carp are bottom feeders for the most part and their mouth is made like a suction cup, so they can suck food off the bottom. Carp are good for a lake because they help clean the bottom of the lake. The largest common carp ever caught in Maryland is a 49-pound fish.

The rainbow trout gets its name because of its brilliant colors. Rainbow trout populations are good indicators of water pollution because they can only survive in clean waters. They like to live in rivers and streams. Rainbow trout rank among the top five most sought game fish in North America. The largest rainbow trout ever caught in Maryland is a 17.44-pound (32-inch) fish.

Brook trout are characterized by their olive-green bodies with pale, worm-like markings, red spots with bluish halos, and orange-red fins with white and black edges. They can grow up to 12 inches in length. Brook trout are cold-water fish that prefer clean, clear, and cold streams, lakes, and ponds. Brook trout generally average 6 to 12 inches in length and weigh between 1/4 to 1 lb.

Tiger trout are known for their aggressive nature and awesome looking tiger-like stripes. Tiger trout are not naturally occurring in the wild, but rather a hybrid created by mixing a female brown trout with a male brook trout. They are stocked in lakes and rivers. Their striking appearance with tiger-like stripes and patterns, makes them easily recognizable. They are known to grow faster than their parent species. Tiger trout typically measure 10–16 inches and weigh 1–3 pounds.

Brown trout can live up to 20 years. Brown trout have a higher tolerance for warmer waters than either brook or rainbow trout. Brown trout can be found on almost every continent except Antarctica, and many can be found living in the ocean. They have olive-brown, yellow-orange, or silvery sides with a mix of black, red, and orange spots. The largest Brown trout ever caught in Maryland weighed 18 pounds, 8 ounces.

The cutthroat's name comes from the bright red or orange slash-like markings under their jaws. There are several subspecies of cutthroat trout, including the coastal, Yellowstone, and Lahontan cutthroat. They inhabit a variety of cold, freshwater environments, including small streams, rivers, and lakes. Mature cutthroat trout can range from 6 to 40 inches in length. The largest cutthroat trout ever caught in Maryland weighed 7 pounds 9 ounces.

Smallmouth bass have a smaller mouth than the largemouth bass. They also have different markings and are lighter in color. They don't live in most lakes because they prefer living in colder water. They are typically found in the northern states in America because the water is cooler. The current world record smallmouth is an 11-pound, 15-ounce fish. They can be found in lakes, reservoirs, and rivers. The largest smallmouth bass ever caught in Maryland weighed 8.2 pounds.

The largemouth bass is the most sought-after bass in North America. Largemouth bass live in just about every lake in North America. They have great hearing and can hear a crayfish crawling on the bottom of the lake. The largest largemouth bass ever caught in Maryland weighed 11 pounds, 6 ounces.

The walleye got its name because of its white looking eyes. Their eyes collect light, even in low light conditions. This means they can see in the dark. Because they can see in the dark, they mostly feed at night. During the daytime their eyes are very sensitive, so they usually head for deeper water or shady places. Walleye like to live in cooler water and are normally found in the upper part of North America. The biggest walleye ever caught in Maryland weighed 14 pounds, 4 ounces.

Pickerel kind of look like northern pike, but they are not. The Pike is larger in size than the Pickerel. The Pickerel has more spots than the Pike, but the Pike has spots on its fins and pickerel don't. Pickerel has a dark bar beneath their eyes and northern pike don't. Pickerel are also known as gunfish or slime darts. The Maryland state record for Chain Pickerel is an 8-pound fish.

The Redfin Pickerel is a small, solitary freshwater fish in the pike family, typically measuring 10–15 inches and living 8–10 years. They inhabit clear, slow-moving, heavily vegetated streams and swamps. They are ambush predators feeding on small fish, crustaceans, and insects. They are olive to yellowish green with distinct, bright red-orange fins and a dark, backwards-slanting bar beneath the eye.

The Northern Pike is one of the most sought-after fish for anglers. It got its name because it likes to live in cooler water mainly in the northern states of North America. The northern pike is a very aggressive predator. They don't like to live in groups with other fish, they are very territorial and like to live alone. Their behavior is closely affected by weather conditions. The biggest Northern Pike ever caught in Maryland weighed 24 pounds, 12 ounces and measured 46 inches long.

The muskellunge called the Musky or Muskie for short is one of the biggest game fish in freshwater lakes. The largest on record was 69 pounds, 15 ounces. The Muskie likes to live in cooler water and can be found in most lakes in the upper part of north America. Anglers look at Muskellunges as trophy fish. They are hard to catch. There's a saying that it takes a thousand casts to catch one. The biggest muskellunge ever caught in Maryland is a 33-pound, 49-inch fish.

Another breed of the Muskie is the tiger muskie. The tiger muskie is a cross between the northern pike and muskie. They grow larger and faster than normal muskies and northern pikes. The tiger muskie got its name because it has tiger like stripes. Tiger Muskies are very rare and hard to catch. The world record tiger muskie is a massive fish weighing 51 pounds, 3 ounces.

Author Page

Billy Grinslott & Kinsey Marie Books

Copyright, All Rights Reserved

ISBN – 9781968228644

Thanks

www.ingramcontent.com/pod-product-compliance
Lightning Source LLC
Chambersburg PA
CBHW040138240726
48664CB00002B/523